# The Rich Farmer

## Nick Butterworth and Mick Inkpen

Marshall Pickering

Here is a farmer who is
very rich. The farmer is rich
because his soil is rich.
And his corn grows faster
than anyone else's.

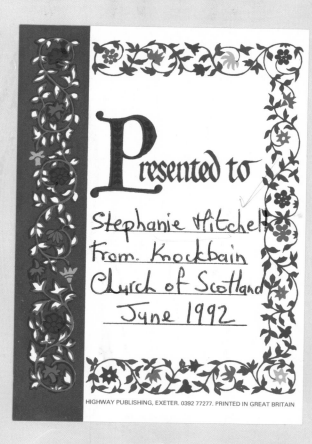

# Presented to

Stephanie Mitchel
From. Knockbain
Church of Scotland
June 1992

HIGHWAY PUBLISHING, EXETER. 0392 77277. PRINTED IN GREAT BRITAIN

Also by Nick Butterworth and Mick Inkpen:

The House on the Rock, The Lost Sheep,
The Two Sons, The Precious Pearl,
The Magpie's Story, The Mouse's Story,
The Fox's Story, The Cat's Story,
I Wonder at the Zoo, I Wonder
on the Farm, I Wonder in the
Country, I Wonder in the Garden.

Copyright © this edition 1992 Nick Butterworth & Mick Inkpen.
First published in 1989 by Marshall Pickering.
Marshall Pickering is an imprint of Harper Collins Religious Division,
Harper Collins Publishers, 77-85 Fulham Palace Road, London W6 8JB, UK.

ISBN 0-551-02508-5

Printed and bound in Hong Kong.

And higher than anyone else's.

And at harvest time he has much more of it than anyone else! Lucky man.

This year he has so much corn
that his old barn can't hold it all.
It is bursting at the seams.

'No problem,' says the farmer.
'I will pull it down and build
a bigger one. Then next year I
will be rich enough to take
life easy.'

So he builds a bigger barn.

But when harvest comes round again, the new barn is not big enough.

The greedy farmer has planted more corn than before. And carrots too.

'No problem,' says the farmer. 'I will build an even bigger, better barn. Then next year I will be richer still and then I can really enjoy myself.'

So he builds a bigger, better barn.

But at harvest time, even the bigger, better barn is not big enough.

Again the farmer has planted too much corn, too many carrots. (And a few cabbages as well.)

This time, the farmer says to himself. 'I will build the biggest, grandest barn the world has ever seen. And then I shall be so rich, I need never work again!'

The barn he builds reaches up to the sky. When it is finished the farmer sighs a great big sigh.

'Tomorrow I will gather in the harvest and then at last I shall begin to enjoy myself. I know! I'll have a party!'

But that very night he dies
in his sleep. Just like that!

The birds eat his corn,
the rabbits dig up his carrots
and his cabbages go to seed.

The big barn stands empty
and the rich farmer never does
get to enjoy his money.

Poor man.

Jesus says, 'How silly it is for a man to spend his whole life storing up riches for himself. To God, he is really a poor man.'